Building a
VIKING SHIP
in Maine

Photo Essay by

PAUL T. CUNNINGHAM

© 2012 Paul T. Cunningham

Cover photographs: © 2012 Paul T. Cunningham.
All photographs are by Paul T. Cunningham.

Decorative elements and engraved illustrations in this book are by Victor R. Lambdin and from *Vikings Tales* by Jennie Hall.

Library of Congress Number: 2011944572

Cunningham, Paul T.
Building a Viking Ship in Maine/ Paul T. Cunningham
p. 158
1.History : Maritime History
2. Transportation : Ships & Shipbuilding - History
I. Title.

ISBN: 978-1-934949-58-0

Published by:

𝔍𝔚𝔅
Just Write Books
Topsham, ME 04086
Printed in the United States of America

Contents

Introduction v

Part One 1

Part Two 17

Part Three 37

Part Four 61

Part Five 91

Part Six 121

Part Seven 129

Part Eight 137

Afterword 142

About the photographer/author 143

Special thanks goes to boat builder Rob Stevens for letting me get in the way so much and to Nicholas Sewall and Lands' End for giving me unlimited access to the project. I have a special remembrance of my late wife during this time while I worked all hours with her support.

Introduction

Snorri, *a Viking Knarr*

Nine men in a wooden boat followed in the wake of Leif Ericsson on a 1,500 mile voyage from Greenland to Newfoundland a thousand years after Leif's great adventure across an unknown sea. Their route took them north from Nuuk, Greenland, along the island's west coast to a shove off point towards the southeast tip of Baffin Island (Leif's Helluland, "flat stone land"), past Labrador Island (Markland, "wood land"), south along the east coast of Newfoundland (Vinland) to L'Anse aux Meadows ("cove in the meadows") on the Great Northern Peninsula of Newfoundland.

Built of oak, pine and locust wood with tamarack for the knees (braces), willow for the trunnels (pegs), and iron rivets, the sailing vessel was christened *Snorri*, namesake of the first child of European parentage to be born in the New World. *Snorri*, son of Thorfinn Karlsefni and his wife, Gudrid, was born ca. 1000 in a Viking settlement on Vinland (now Newfoundland).

The lead builder of the Viking ship reproduction was Rob Stevens, who was contracted by W. Hodding Carter, expedition leader of Viking Voyage 1000, as the project was called. The sole sponsor was Lands' End Direct Merchants, a catalog retailer. Boatbuilders Robert Miller and Dave Foster and cabinetmaker Scott Smith assisted Stevens. Later, other talented craftsmen joined the project to help meet the deadline. Gerry Galuza, a renown blacksmith, produced the 2,700 handmade iron rivets. *Snorri* was constructed in seven months' time on Hermit Island in Phippsburg, a town on a peninsula, or point, of Midcoast Maine.

Snorri was modeled after Skuldelev Wreck No. 1, a Viking merchant ship skuddled ca. 1000 in Roskilde, Denmark. Measuring 54 feet long, 16 feet wide and 6 feet deep with an open deck, the original vessel was a *knarr*, a boat designed for ocean voyages and hauling cargo for trade. It did not have the speed and agility of a Viking attack longboat. Empty, *Snorri* weighed 12 tons but sailed with a ballast of 13 tons of rock. For power, *Snorri* relied on the wind in its canvas sail and its crew at its six oars.

The first test of *Snorri's* seaworthiness began July 16, 1997, but ended with the failure of the rudder's framing, which in rough seas caused damage to the overlapped single-layer strakes (planks) where the rudder was affixed, which resulted in water leakage. The boat had to be dry docked in Nuuk for repair and the voyage delayed.

The second attempt to follow Lief Ericsson's lead shoved off June 28, 1998, from Nuuk, Greenland, with a new rudder assembly designed by Stevens after he visited the Viking museum in Roskilde for ideas and suggestions. Snorri arrived successfully September 22, 1998, with the crew wading ashore at L'anse aux Meadows, Newfoundland.

L'Anse aux Meadows is a Canadian National Historic Site and a UNESCO World Heritage Site. Excavations have revealed the footprint and some remains of wood-framed buildings (8 houses, 4 workshops, 1 forge) made of peat-turf that were similar to structures of Norse construction of the same period that have been found in Greenland and Iceland. The site is considered to be evidence of the earliest European presence in the New World and the oldest European-style settlement found in America. The dig area, called the Epaves Bay archeology site, had been first identified in 1960 by Helge Ingstad and Anne Stine Ingstad, who had followed clues in medieval Icelandic manuscripts and Viking sagas to locate the settlement area. Anne Stine Ingstad led the excavations from 1961 to 1968 and Parks Canada took the lead from 1973 to 1976.

On September 22, 1998, the day the vessel arrived in Newfoundland, *Snorri* was donated to Norstead Village Inc. in L'Anse aux Meadows by The New Vinland Foundation, which had been founded by Carter to foster education about Viking lore and achievements, something that had enthralled him as a child.

Through his skillful use of light and camera, photographer Paul Cunningham has caught the action of building a Viking ship from stem post to stern post and a contemporary view of modern men making preparation to go a-viking in pursuit of adventure, knowledge and a successful voyage — treasures worth far more than silver and gold.

Sources:

"L'Anse aux Meadows," <whc.unesco.org>, UNESCO, 2011.

"L'Anse aux Meadows National Historic Site of Canada," <www.pc.gc.ca>, 24 April 2009.

"Leif Ericsson," <www.viking.no/e/people/leif>, The Viking Network, 15 April 2000.

"Viking Voyage 1000 - The Story of *Snorri* the Knarr - Adventure, Lands' End," <www.dougcabot.com/ship/vi_building.html>, Doug Cabot, ca. 1998.

"Visit the *Snorri* Viking Ship," <www.norstead.com>, Norstead Village Inc., undated.

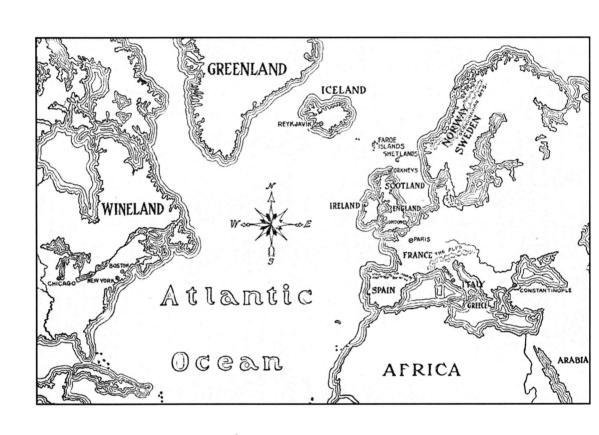

Building a
VIKING SHIP
in Maine

Part One

Phippsburg boat builder Rob Stevens begins shaping a piece of oak with his trusty adze.

David Foster shapes the keel of the vessel.

Foster in silhouette working at the bow end of the keel.
Behind him are Robert Miller, left, and Scott Smith.

Rob Stevens shapes the aft stem of the vessel. Near him
are several of the molds that soon will be attached to
the keel.

Scott Smith, left, and David Foster attach the first boat
mold to the keel.

Rob Stevens uses a pulley to lift the aft stem into position. Scott Smith, left, and David Foster center and steady the piece.

Another view of the first mold as seen from inside the boatshop.

Rob Stevens works at the aft end of the vessel.

Scott Smith and David Foster attach more molds to the keel.

The bow stem post.

During the construction process, visitors often made
their way into the Hermit Island boatshop.

Once all the molds have been put in position, the size and shape of the vessel become apparent.

Rob Stevens, left, high school student "Topher" Homan, and Scott Smith attach one of the final molds near the bow stem.

A temporary addition to the boatshop was created to accommodate the 54-foot vessel.

Part Two

David Foster shapes one of the first yellow pine planks that will be used for the clinker built or lapstrake hull.

A close-up photo shows planks and the rounded top of the keel.

Scott Smith works near the aft section of the boat as the
planking begins.

David Foster, left, and Rob Stevens plank the hull.

Stevens pulls a piece of yellow pine from his custom-made steamer. The hot steam makes the wood more pliable.

Robert Miller, left, and Rob Stevens fit a large piece of
pine to the molds.

Numerous clamps are used to secure the plank in position.

Robert Miller planes a plank.

Apparently, Miller needs to watch his head when near this mold.

30   Scott Smith heats handcrafted rivets outside the shop.

Once heated, the rivets are dunked in warm pine tar.

Rivets and roves connect the planks.

Woolwich blacksmith Gerry Galuza prepares his fire.

Right: Galuza scores a strip of roves. For this project, Galuza's shop created more than 2,700 rivets and roves for the vessel.

The stern stem takes shape.

The rivets and roves hold together the hull planks. Scott
Smith adds another plank.

Scott Smith brushes a mix of pine tar and linseed oil onto the planks. The mixture is a sealant and preservative that boat builders have used for centuries.

Part Three

Another piece of southern yellow pine is planed into a hull plank.

David Foster uses a modern router to shape a floor timber. "If the Viking's had one, they would have used it."

John Gardner marks a slab of oak frame stock before
cutting it.

David Foster and Scott Smith cut a floor timber on the
band saw.

Deirdre Whitehead uses a drill press to clean the center
of the roves.

John Gardner, left, Deirdre Whitehead, and Scott Smith
have lunch under racks of drying willow used for trunnel
stock. Hundreds of trunells were used in the making of
the viking boat *Snorri*.

In early January, Robert Miller celebrates a birthday
with the help of his wife, Alison Hepler, and boat-
building friends.

The hull begins to take shape.

David Foster planes excess wood from a large piece of
oak that will become a floor timber. Nearby is the pattern
he used.

A look, from the stern to the bow, of the molds and their reinforcements.

David Foster makes a pattern on a piece oak before cutting the wood.

Scott Smith fits a floor timber into place.

Work continues on the inside and outside of the hull.

W. Hodding Carter visits the shop in January to check the progress on the vessel. During Carter's visit, John Gardner, back to camera, asks to be a member of the crew.

David Dick shapes treenails, otherwise known as trenails
or trunnels, by hand.

A box of willow treenails ready for use.

Rob Stevens carves a piece of wood for use as the mast
step. Vikings referred to this part of the ship as the
keelson or "The Old Woman."

The stockpile of oak and hackmatack near the boatshop.

John Gardner carefully checks a piece of oak.

Occasionally the winter high tides made getting to the shop more challenging. Rob Stevens said he knew that I would probably visit on the days of such flood tides.

A Viking ship cutout sits on the window sill.

Part Four

The outside of the hull nears completion.

Inside the hull, floor timbers, knees, bites and frames are carefully shaped and secured.

A photo taken from inside the hull showing the aft section and deck beams.

Above: John Gardner finishes a breast hook for the
bow of the knarr.

Upper left: A side frame is fitted into place.

Left: As the launch date nears, a new sign to
minimize interruptions is placed outside the door
of the shop near rough hackmatack knees.

Robert Miller carves a side frame.

Rob Stevens takes a break.

Robert Miller finishes a side frame.

This photo shows the six-foot depth of the hull.

David Dick drives a treenail, or trunnel, into the hull.

Nearing launch date, the builders forge ahead, shaping
the remaining knees and frames of the knarr.

WE ARE SEARCHING FOR A PIECE OF HARDWOOD GROWN TO THIS SHAPE. WE NEED IT IMMEDIATELY FOR THE KNARR PRESENTLY UNDER CONSTRUCTION. — ROBERT STEVENS BOATBUILDER. (207) 389-1794

Upper left: Another new sign, this one asking for a unique piece of wood.

Lower left: Rob Stevens shapes the stern hook with his adze. "Sometimes in wooden boat building, the older tools are the right ones to use."

Below: Stevens and the other builders continue on the inside of the hull.

Deirdre Whitehead works on the "dead eyes" for
the rigging.

With the launch just a few days away, Scott Smith
shapes the rudder.

Launch chains and pulleys are readied.

The mast in an early stage (*top*) and, later, finished and
ready to be used (*bottom*).

The inside of the vessel after a good vacuuming.

The addition to the shop is removed.

The boat builders gather around W. Hodding Carter, his wife, Lisa Lattes, and their twin daughters Anabel and Eliza for a group photo. Also participating were two canine mascots.

The area outside the shop is cleaned for the big day.

For the first time, the stern of the knarr basks in
sunlight.

The builders enjoy a farewell lunch together. After the
launching, some will be off on new adventures.

David Miller assembles the crib under the knarr.

Part Five

On the day of the launch, Skip Foster, David's son,
uses a powerful winch to begin moving the vessel,
toward the water stern first.

An old Ford truck provides the power to move the knarr
toward the incoming tide as Rob Stevens give directions.

Boards and skids are placed under the crib as the truck's winch draws the vessel along.

A bumper sticker claims that the truck is not an
abandoned vehicle.

Docks, stacked from the previous winter, provide an excellent view of the launching for a documentary camera crew.

The vessel approaches the water's edge.

The last boards and skids are placed. Two metal pipes, used as rollers, can be seen under the boat.

Rob Stevens puts on a pair of hip boots, preparing
for a better view of the launch.

Rob Stevens wades into the ocean to check the hull.

A group of people wait, watch and try to "will" the tide in.

Passing the oars aboard.

Boat builders John Gardner, left, and David Foster take
a break.

Above: A bouquet of flowers is attached to the bow post
by James Murdock.

Right: A helicopter circles overhead as the crowd awaits
the launch. Owing to shop isolation, a limited number of
people are allowed to visit on launch day.

A crowd of well-wishers watch as the knarr floats into
water of the cove.

The craftsmen, future crew and families take the knarr for
a trial row.

Above: The cove gets crowded.

Upper right: W. Hodding Carter talks to some of the visitors after the shakedown cruise.

Lower right: Blacksmith Gerry Galuza wears a "Viking" helmet for the occasion.

After a successful cruise around the cove,
visitors inspect the knarr.

With the knarr removed, mast, rope and other rigging fill
the workshop.

The vessel is tied up at Hermit Island, awaiting the mast and several thousand pounds of ballast.

The boat as seen from West Point, Maine, as the crew
practices sea drills.

Part Six

The launching at Hermit Island allowed only limited
access. A christening ceremony was scheduled at the
Maine Maritime Museum in Bath.

W. Hodding Carter addresses the crowd at the museum.

Builders share a few laughs as the ceremony begins.

The crowd at the christening ceremony.

Rob Stevens takes his turn at the mike.

As the opening remarks continue, the builders reluctantly step up for their well-deserved recognition.

The media was out in force.

After the vessel receives her name, *Snorri*, visitors gather
to see her up close.

Part Seven

Ballast loaded and the rigging in place,
crewmen work on their navigation computer.
As was often said on site, "If the Vikings had
one, they would have used it."

John Gardner works on the rudder.

After the launching and christening, Rob Stevens returns to his boatshop to finish preparing other boats for the summer ahead.

The crew later sailed *Snorri* to Boston, where she was packed on a container ship. After several transfers from one ship to another, *Snorri* arrived in Brattahlid, Greenland, followed by W. Hodding Carter, Rob Stevens, John Gardner and the rest of the crew.

When ready, Snorri and her crew sailed down a fiord toward Cape Desolation. On July 29, 1997, they reached open sea and headed up the west coast of Greenland toward Sisimiut. That night an iceberg suddenly loomed in the distance, and, as Stevens recalls, it was the only time during the adventure that he was truly nervous.

As they neared the halfway point of the Davis Strait, the frame that the rudder rope was tied to suddenly pulled forward, opening four one-inch holes in the hull where trunnels had been. Later that same evening the rudder line broke, disabling the crew's ability to steer.

After talking with the Coast Guard, it was decided that a tow back to Greenland was the safest alternative and that they would try again the next summer.

Part Eight

Rob Stevens, W. Hodding Carter and Terry Moore work on rudder alterations for the second attempt to sail from Greenland to Newfoundland.

Once the design was agreed on, Stevens began carving
the new rudder.

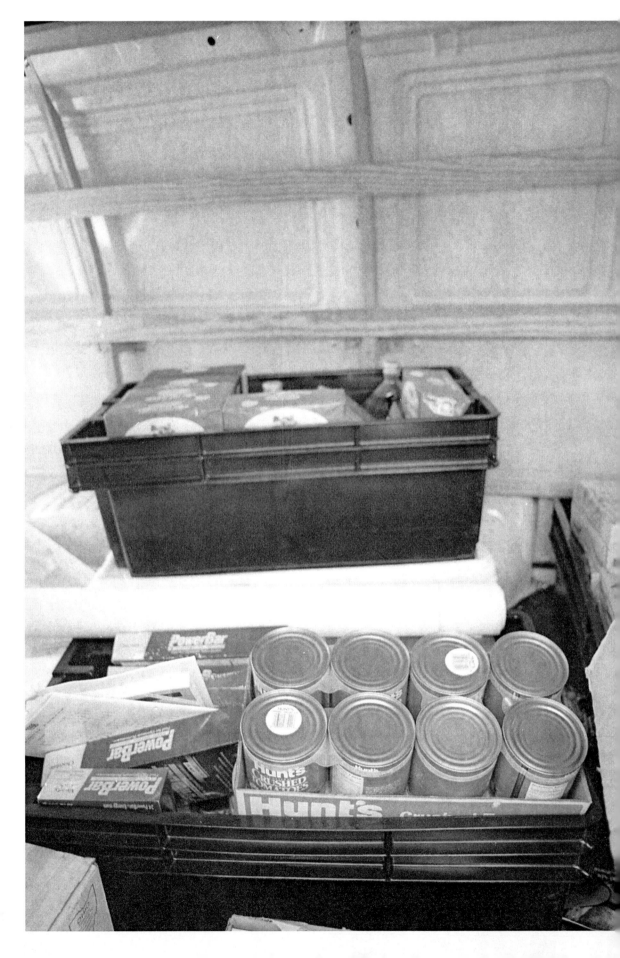

Food and footwear for the next voyage.

Afterword

After setting sail from Nuuk, Greenland, on June 28, 1998, the crew successfully navigated the Davis Strait and on September 22, 1998, landed at L'Anse aux Meadows, Newfoundland. *Snorri* was then donated to the Viking Trail Tourism Association to be used as a permanent display at the L'Anse aux Meadows National Historic Site.

Paul T. Cunningham

Paul T. Cunningham grew up in Freeport, Maine. He earned a degree in Secondary Science Education at University of Southern Maine (Gorham State College). Subsequently, for nearly a decade, he taught elementary science in Gardiner, Maine.

Paul's love of photography led him away from the classroom. His first photographic job was with *The Shopping Notes* during the late 1980s. In 1990 Cunningham began his career as photojournalist at *The Times Record* and retired from there in 2008. Now Paul freelances, and volunteers with Freeport Fire and Rescue and the Freeport Historical Society. The balance of his time is spent organizing the fruits of two decades of photography.

CPSIA information can be obtained at www.ICGtesting.com
Printed in the USA
BVOW080527080312

284670BV00002B/2/P